Christ and The Cutter

A Christian Guide to Understanding Self Harm and How to Help Healing Today

Aaron Mamuyac

Copyright 2016 by Aaron Mamuyac
Researched and written by Aaron Mamuyac

All rights reserved. Without limiting the rights under the copyright reserved above, no part of this publication may be reproduced, stored in, or introduced into a retrieval system, or transmitted in any form or by any means (electronic, mechanical, photocopying, recording, or otherwise) without prior written permission.

For permission requests, please contact:
aaron@sunlightcc.org

ISBN-13:
978-1533566409

ISBN-10:
1533566402

While every effort has been made to ensure the accuracy and legitimacy of the references, referrals, and links (collectively "Links") presented in this e-book, Aaron Mamuyac is not responsible or liable for broken Links or missing or fallacious information at the Links. Any Links in this e-book to a specific product, process, website, or service do not constitute or imply an endorsement by Aaron of same, or its producer or provider. The views and opinions contained in any Links do not necessarily express or reflect those of Aaron Mamuyac.

Dedication

This book is dedicated to my youth group. You guys deal with so much, and I wish you didn't have to. But my prayer and hope is that struggles and trials in life only drive you deeper into a relationship with Jesus. Love you guys.

Table of Contents

Introduction 1
Chapter 1 - What is Self-Harm? 7
Chapter 2 - The Cycle of Addiction 11
Chapter 3 - Different Modes of Self-harm 16
Chapter 4 - Why Do People Self-harm? 23
Chapter 5 - Understanding Family Dynamics 28
Chapter 6 - Understanding Our Role 33
Chapter 7 - Relational Recovery............................ 40
Chapter 8 - Action Steps 45
Epilogue 49
Free Video – Examples and Understanding Suicidal Thoughts... 51
I'd Love to Hear from You! 52
About the Author 53

Introduction

Do you know someone who is addicted to cutting?
Do you feel uneducated about self-harm?
Do you feel inadequate to help?
Do want to be equipped and to feel competent enough to help those who harm themselves find a path to recovery?
If you answered yes to any of these questions, then this book is for you.

This book aims to help you quickly understand self-harm and to equip you to help hurting people efficiently.

Talking openly helps educate people and grow awareness. As a society, we speak freely about sexuality, racism, and politics, as well as many other controversial topics. Subjects that used to be taboo are not anymore.

However, one thing we still do not talk about often enough is self-harm. As a result, we fail to truly understand it. We have misconceptions about what self-harm is. Our society still regards it as taboo. As a result, thousands suffering from this addiction are hindered from finding help.

What does a self-harmer look like?

Self-harming kids aren't "Ghoulish Frankensteins" preoccupied with blood and gore. They are artists, actors, and athletes. They are regular kids, deeply hurting, overwhelmed by their emotions. Emotional management is why they cut. When they discover cutting doesn't work and desire to stop, they find that they can't. Did you know that most people who self-harm want to quit?

How do we help?

The #1 reason why people can't help someone who self-injures is because they don't know why someone self injures.

This eBook seeks to educate you about self-harm, the reasons behind it, and how best to treat those who resort to it. It's scary. It might be confusing, and you might have no idea how to even think about it. "How could someone do that?" I want to shed some light on why people cut themselves and motivate you to help them move past it as early as today.

Let's talk some statistics.

- Did you know that in 1998 cutting was an admitted issue for 1 in 250 girls and 0 guys?
- In 2006 cutting is now admitted by 1 in 5 girls and 1 in 7 guys.
- About 90% of those who self-injure began their behavior as teenagers.
- The average self-injurers starts at age 14 and continues with increasing severity into his or her late 20's.
- There is evidence that some self-injury could be a "learned behavior." (This means that is could be contagious.)

My point with all these statistics is this: **There are people who are hurting, and we need to educate ourselves in order to help.**

"I don't know what I am doing. Even if I wanted to help, I wouldn't know how!"

I have been in youth ministry for 10 years. In that time, many students have shared their stories about cutting with me. As I listened, I felt inadequate – unable to think of anything to say in response. I felt like I lacked knowledge and the ability to help for them. I didn't know what to say or do. I couldn't understand them. It was hard for me to sympathize with them.

I am writing this book for people who feel the same way.

I want to encourage you and to say that you can help the people you love. You don't have to be unaware or ignorant of this phenomenon anymore. With proper information and this step-by-step guide to understanding self-harm, you can help bring recovery and healing to those who need it most!

Now let's talk about healing.

The only true and full healing for hurting teens is in the Christian worldview.

I believe that Christianity offers the only real healing for self-harmers. Therapy only takes a person so far. The causes of cutting are deep and can only be fully solved in the healing work of the Gospel and the cross of Christ. The therapist only deals with part of the problem, but it is the theologian that sees the whole reality.

Professional help, techniques, and therapy alone cannot truly heal someone lost in self-harm.

This book seeks to bring true healing to self-injurers by examining how the Christian worldview answers their needs. You will learn how to help someone who self-harms find true healing, and true healing only comes from Jesus Christ.

The Bible teaches how Jesus understood the deep underlying needs of humanity. We all need purpose and meaning to our lives. We all want security and a sense of belonging. We want to be loved by someone, and we want a life with hope and a future.

For someone who self-harms, they feel like they are missing these things in their life. The feelings become more and more intense, and they become overwhelmed. Modern therapy cannot deliver love. Self-motivation cannot do enough. But Jesus can, and he has demonstrated his love for us on the cross.

On the cross, Jesus fills us with purpose and meaning to life. He saves us and takes us into a relationship with himself. When we have hit rock bottom, we will realize that Jesus is the rock at the bottom. From there the Bible tells us we have hope and a future.

Jesus turns the victim into the victor and assures us that there is purpose on the other side of the pain.

He wants you to play a part in his rescue plan for his children, and now you can. This short guide will help you be the bridge God will use between Christ and the Cutter.

I believe a great passage for us to reflect on when trying to help those who are hurting is a promise found in Isaiah 61. We should be reminded and empowered to know that God is the healer and that we are not. We don't need to carry the burden of obtaining results. It's not our spirit that rescues, but the Holy Spirit.

As you read this passage, think about the good news that we bring. Think about the poor we minister to. Remember that 'poor' is more than money or financial status. It also means spiritual health. Picture those who are broken hearted, imprisoned, and bound up. Now remember the God of Ages, the Creator of the Universe, the Healer of the Sick, the Good Shepard, and the Perfect Father. The one who is greater than us will do great things through us. That is His promise.

Isaiah 61:1-4
The Spirit of the Lord God is upon me,

    because the Lord has anointed me
to bring good news to the poor;
    he has sent me to bind up the brokenhearted,
to proclaim liberty to the captives,
    and the opening of the prison to those who are bound;
to proclaim the year of the Lord's favor,
    and the day of vengeance of our God;
    to comfort all who mourn;
to grant to those who mourn in Zion—
    to give them a beautiful headdress instead of ashes,
the oil of gladness instead of mourning,
    the garment of praise instead of a faint spirit;
that they may be called oaks of righteousness,
    the planting of the Lord, that he may be glorified.
They shall build up the ancient ruins;
    they shall raise up the former devastations;
they shall repair the ruined cities,
    the devastations of many generations.

Part One
Understanding the Addiction

Chapter 1 - What is Self-Harm?

Lesson Overview
In this lesson, we will discuss what self-harm is, what it is not, and where those who harm themselves can find hope.

Defining Self-harm
Self-harm has a lot of names, including self-injury, self-inflicted violence, and non-suicide self-injury (NSSI). It is the practice of cutting or injuring one's self, usually indicating a psychological disturbance. Self-harm does not usually occur in groups, but alone and in secret. It is a cry for help, an escape, an expression, a destructive way to cope, a way to manage emotions, and a sign of deeper unfulfilled critical needs.

What self-harm is NOT
Self-harm is not self-mutilation! This is the most common misconception. Kids cut to make things better. It is Emotional Management. In the mind of the person who is doing it, it is about self-care not self-mutilation. Self-mutilation comes from a place of wanting things to be worse than they are. Self-harm comes from wanting a better reality.

Self-injury is not a halfhearted attempt at suicide. The lie that kids believe is that self-harm promises emotional management, emotional relief, peace, and calm. Teens cut because they treasure life and want it to be better. Because of this, self-harm is doomed to fail. It cannot give the lasting relief that they seek. Only when the promises of self-harm start to fail will they turn to suicide. In their mind, self-injury is seen as a temporary solution to what feels like a permanent problem. When the pain doesn't go away, then they will see suicide as a permanent solution to what may be a temporary problem. Cutting is not suicide initially, but it can lead a person to the point eventually.

<u>Self-harm is not body modification taken to an extreme</u>. Body modification is driven by uniqueness. The goal is looking for a desired reaction from people. They are most likely trying to manage how people interact with them. When someone wants a tattoo or pierces their body, they don't like the pain, but it comes with the tattoo. Most would prefer the tattoo without the pain. For people who cut themselves, the pain is the goal for the self-harmer. **It is the calming effect on their lives that they crave**.

<u>Self-harm is not demon possession</u>. If it was, all we would have to do is bring a priest in with a cross and some holy water. Is there spiritual warfare involved? Yes, absolutely. The spiritual war being waged comes in the form of believing lies instead of the truth. It is accepting self-doubt and the accusations of Satan over the awareness of being a child of God. It is where the noise of the devil muffles out the whisper of love from our heavenly Father.

<u>Self-harm is not a relationally immature attempt at getting attention</u>. It is not an adolescent attempting to get attention. Attention-seeking behavior occurs in insecure people who want an excessive and unneeded amount of attention. The best reaction we should have to attention-seeking behavior is to simply ignore it. However, we should never ignore self-harm. If attention-getting behavior is used to demand more attention than needed, self-harm is used to RIGHTFULLY demand more attention where it should be. Cutting then becomes a person's legitimate and painful cry for an someone else to be involved in their life when they are not.

Hope in Self-harm

Self-harm is NOT hopeless. We can end the cycle of hurt. There is a way of overcoming this practice, although it can seek unbreakable. There are a lot of conventional methods that claim to bring healing. One such suggestion is creating art, such as painting or drawings, as a healthier way to express emotions. Journaling is also often clinically prescribed. Reaching out to others and finding another person to whom they can be accountable is also a common treatment. What has been shown, however, is that these will all fail eventually. These are not a surefire way to end self-harming behavior. These are good habits but not what a self-injurer ultimately needs.

Although I support all those techniques as healthy alternatives, these are just Band-Aids to the real problem. A person who is resorting to self-harm does not have a problem with lack of expressive options; they have an issue with a lack of love. A lack of value. A lack of self-worth. They fail to see their significance.

I believe only the Christian worldview offers the tools we need to offer true healing. Christianity diagnoses the real problem as spiritual. It is a lack of love, a sense of abandonment, and an experience of hopelessness and emptiness. Reality lines up with the Bible when we observe that the most common reasons teens give for cutting are typically variations on four themes:

> 1. "Why did this evil happen to me?"
> 2. "Where is justice, and who can make it right?"
> 3. "How can I find forgiveness?"
> 4. "Who could love someone as broken as me?"

Evil. Justice. Forgiveness. Love.

Christianity teaches that all these deep questions were answered on a hill called Calvary in the person and work of Jesus Christ. Jesus bore the weight of all of the worst kinds evil. He was punished for the guilty to answer the demand for justice. Jesus extends forgiveness for a future, and he loves broken and messy people, who he welcomes into his family.

This is good news. (Christianity calls it the Gospel). Because of Jesus' innocent death, we can find answers to our most painful questions. Isaiah 53:5 talks about how we are healed by His wounds.

Isaiah 53:5
But He was wounded for our transgressions,
He was bruised for our iniquities;
The chastisement of our peace was upon Him,
And by His stripes, we are healed.

Chapter 2 - The Cycle of Addiction

Lesson Overview
In this lesson, we will discuss how addiction works with the "Road to Addiction" Chart.

The Lie of Addictive Behavior
Every addictive behavior begins with a promise:

"If you drink, you will be cool."
"If you smoke, people will like you."
"If you cut, all the craziness will go away."

In the early stages, destructive behaviors may seem to deliver on their promises. When we drink, people are intrigued and it makes us cool. When we smoke, we may gain a few friends. It does temporarily take the pain away, and it makes us feel good.

However, these behaviors quickly move to a place where they cannot continue to deliver on their promises. The high wears off and the excitement dies down. The positive effects are temporary and short-lived.

When that happens, the next logical step is to do it again. We try to relive the same fun escape. What always happens, however, is that we will experience the same drop. So we do it again. And again. And again. Now we are in a place where we are defined by the behavior. This is the cycle of addiction.

The Path to Addiction

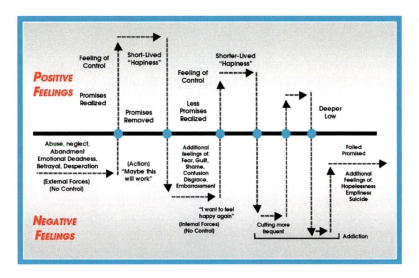

Let's discuss the chart. The chart is split up into two sections which represent the two emotions people feel: positive (top) and negative (bottom) feelings.

People who are prone to addictive behavior have a bigger negative space. This is due to biological factors such as genetics and/or circumstantial factors such as quality of home life. This includes experiences of abuse, neglect, abandonment, and betrayal that lead to emotional deadness and desperation.

To deal with their circumstances and feelings, people stumble into self-harming behavior that launches them into the realm of positive emotions.

Again, the promise of the behavior is to offer control over the way they feel, which is incredibly important because they feel that the situations in their life are out of their control. The act of cutting only gives someone the illusion of control only for a little while. A "short-lived" feeling of happiness (or relief/reprieve) is experienced, but then a plunge into depression follows. Reality sets in, and they realize that their circumstances did not change. They remember the way they feel. Everything is back to the way it was.

However, it is actually worse. They now experience the additional feelings of fear, guilt, and shame because they have indulged in cutting. Additionally, they feel confusion, disgrace, and embarrassment because they didn't know how to deal with their emotions. All they remembered was that they escaped for a short time. Then they repeat the cycle, as they return to the behavior.

As we move from left to right on the Path to Addiction, you will notice that the jump into the positive feelings is reduced after each time they cut. The time spent in the escape is shorter. The dive into depression is deeper and stronger. The cutting will become more frequent as the law of diminishing returns settles in. This is when addiction happens.

This law of diminishing returns can be seen in other destructive behaviors. People get drunk and have a great time one night, so they do it again. For a short time they forget about the things in life that cause anxiety.

Then they repeat the actions to get a repeat of the same experiences and emotions. What ends up happening is they try to change it up and add variety to keep the emotions high. They will go to different club, drink different liquor, do it with different friends. But there is only so much variety you can add until they find that this pattern of behavior (any pattern really) will eventually run dry. Now because they have done this for so long, why stop? They believe it is who they are now.

The Goal Has Changed
Addiction to cutting happens the same way. It happens when the goal moves from being about pleasure-seeking to being purely about managing pain. At this point compounding feelings of guilt, shame, hurt, brokenness, and emptiness keep on piling up, while the circumstances or past experiences haven't been dealt with.

When the promise of cutting doesn't propel them into their positive emotions or escape anymore, despair sets in. Most turn to more severe forms of self-harm. They think that perhaps changing it up, trying something new, or making it hurt more will bring that escape again.

This is why it is important to notice the different modes of self-harm. This path leads down to more intense forms of self-injury. This is how suicide becomes an alternative. They have tried everything, and nothing works anymore to manage their pain. They are tired of the endless cycle of management, and all they want is rest.

Outside Strength to Break Addiction
The reality is that to break addiction you need outside help. We are not strong enough on our own to break an addiction. This is the very reason why counselors, therapists, 12-step programs, and halfway houses exist. Rehab clinics and former addicts would echo this statement. People need outside help.

Christianity teaches that the true strength to break the chains of addiction is found only in Jesus. He has given us the Holy Spirit, who has the power to move us from a destructive lifestyle to a vibrant life lived with him.

It is imperative that we show that no life is hopeless. Every life can be turned around. We don't have to white knuckle our own freedom. Strength, freedom, and the ability to stand and live again are found in God. He is faithful to see us through it.

He promises us that he will keep temptations that we cannot handle away from us. This means that, whatever temptations we find in front of us, God is with us, and he is faithful to see us through it.

1 Corinthians 10:13
No temptation has seized you except what is common to man. And God is faithful; he will not let you be tempted beyond what you can bear. But when you are tempted, he will also provide a way out so that you can stand up under it.

Chapter 3 - Different Modes of Self-harm

Lesson Overview
In this chapter, we will take a look at the various types of self-harm.

Men and women self-harm differently. All are done in seclusion and privacy, which makes the behavior hard to address. It is important what we are familiar with the various methods of self-harm so that we reduce the shock of discovery and are familiar with treatments.

Alcohol
Alcohol is used by many people to assist them in relieving feelings and emotions that can be overwhelming. It is a way of self-harm that's barely given a second look. However, the very fact remains that it is a way of self-harm that may lead to instant harm, or it may end in semi-permanent damage. It could lead to liver damage or ulcers. Often alcohol is combined drugs or medications, which can lead to overdosing.

Burning
Burning skin is a method of self-injury that was seen in 12.9% of students who self-harmed. Another alternative that is common is heating up the top of a lighter by letting the flame stay lit and then stamping the top of the lighter onto the skin creating a 'C' branding.

Cutting
Whereas cutting is commonly thought of as synonymous with self-harm, this manner of self-injury only occurred in about 1-in-3 students who reported self-harming. Cutting is more common among females, but it is not exclusive to them. This is often what people typically consider when they say somebody "self-harms." Cutting is

commonly done as a "release," but in some instances it may be done as a form of punishment as well. Cuts may vary in severity, depending on the need of the cutter. Cuts are usually on the forearm, thighs or places where they might be hidden. Some cutters will go to great lengths to cover up what they are doing.

In the case of those who have been the victim of rape or molestation, cuts might be made to breasts and genitals. The most common and dangerous cuts are those that move up on the wrist. The ensuing harm is typically more immediate than in other kinds of self-harm. Cutting isn't a suicide attempt, but it should not be seen as less imperative to address.

Carving
Carving is another manner of self-harm in which someone carves words or symbols into the skin. This is what cutting evolves into. This is where the cut speaks. Words like "ugly," "fat," empty," "mom," and "dad" are the cries of someone in despair.

Embedding
This kind of self-harm involves the rubbing of sharp objects, like glass, into the skin. Twelve percent of responding students used this manner to self-harm. This is taken further when an incision is made in the skin and glass is inserted. Then they wait for time to pass so that it heals over. Now whenever overwhelming feelings take over, the self-harmer punches that spot. Instant bruising will occur. This is extremely dangerous because of internal damage and infection.

Food Abuse
This includes binge feeding, deliberate starvation, and purging (vomiting). Food is used as self-harm to regulate emotions. This often reflects a distain for one's own body image. Gorging and binging will relieve feelings of

emptiness (wanting to be filled) while purging can release feelings that were bottled up (wanting to get something out of them).

More serious ways of "eating for harm" involve ingesting non-food or chemicals. Aside from the plain instant relief of feeling full or empty, using food as a way of self-harm is a technique for making the feeling of harm last longer.

Impact with Objects
This self-harm behavior involves banging, punching objects, or one's self for bruising or trauma. This manner of self-harm was admitted in 25% of people. Sitting and banging one's head against the wall is typically associated with frustration and inner hurt and is more commonly seen in males (but not exclusively).

Medicine/Drugs
This is the misuse of illegal and legal drugs, including prescribed medications, over-the-counter medications or substances from aerosols, gas, or glue. Drugs fulfill a spread of wishes and illicit or blocked feelings that are too overwhelming if one isn't in an altered state of mind. The short-term and long-term risks are high. Drug use is extremely dangerous.

Ripped Skin
This manner of self-injury includes tearing the skin. This sort of self-injury was seen in 16% of these who admitted for self-harming behaviors.

Interfering with Healing
This manner of self-injury is commonly seen in combination with other styles of self-harm. The person purposefully hampers the healing of wounds, and 13.5% of respondents admitted to this method of self-harm.

Scratching or Pinching
This behavior involves severely scratching or pinching with fingernails or objects for the purpose of making marks on the skin or causing bleeding. This technique of self-injury was seen in more than half all
students who reported participating in self-harm.

Trichotillomania
Another mode of self-harm is medically referred to as trichotillomania. In trichotillomania, a person feels compelled to pull out their own hair and in some cases ingest that hair. In the United States, there are over 200,000 reported cases per year.

General Observations
There are still many more types of self-harm. People who self-harm need help to find different ways of expressing themselves when the tsunami of emotions overtakes them. This behavior happens when they are alone, so it is hard to stop them unless you are with them all the time. This is why developing a relationship with them is crucial. They need to feel comfortable enough to tell you when they self harm. We will discuss how we can accomplish this in Part Three.

When we become informed of a loved one engaging in self-harm, we can misunderstand the severity of it. We might believe it isn't that bad, or think that it's just a phase. One of the worst things we can do is misdiagnose the severity of their behavior.

We need to be able to correctly diagnose the situation so that we can correctly address it and make significant steps toward recovery. If we fail to see the situation accurately, we will fail to help them.

The Diagnosis of the Healer

In the book of Jeremiah, God sees his people suffering and in pain. However, he sees that the priests, prophets, and ministers who are in charge do not take it seriously. They do not see the situation for what it really is. The ones who are supposed to bring healing misdiagnose the problem and take it too lightly. They say everything is all right when its not.

But God sees the deepest pain in all its fullness and makes an astonishing remark. He addresses the priests and ministers that were chosen to represent him and bring healing and rebukes them. He says how they do not see the full picture. In this little verse in Jeremiah, God identifies the error of misdiagnosing the severity of a problem. God says, "Don't say there is peace and happiness when there isn't any." We shouldn't either.

One reason why we fail to see harmful behaviors is that it makes us feel uncomfortable. Recognizing a behavior in a self-harmer means dealing with it. We shouldn't ignore the suffering of someone else because it makes us uncomfortable. We should correctly identify it.

God correctly deals with our sins, but first he had to diagnose our life.

Jeremiah 6:14
They dress the wounds of my people as though it were not serious. "Peace, peace," they say when there is no peace.

Part Two
Understanding the Motivations

Chapter 4 - Why Do People Self-harm?

Lesson Overview
In this lesson, we will discuss the different reasons why people self-harm.

Cause
The most common cause for why young people to self-harm is the pain that comes specifically from broken relationships where trust has been betrayed. Betrayal. It is when a relationship that should be loving and trustworthy has turned into a source of pain. A relationship that has turned dangerous instead of protective. A relationship that should be nurturing feels empty. Children need to feel safe. They need to feel loved. They need a sense of value and worth. Removing any one of these factors will be extremely detrimental to the development of the person.

Incest. Rape. Murder. Abandonment. Neglect. Physical and verbal abuse. Addictions. Denial. Slavery. These are all evils that today's children might find themselves victims of. Family structures are in place so that children are shielded from these things. However, when someone in the family betrays the structure, the sense of security and stability is lost. Identity is shaken, and worth is challenged.

As a result, they grow into their teen years with low self-esteem and start self-harming to cope. They constantly compare themselves to others, and they are at the bottom. Self-harmers have a lifetime of stuffed emotions. They might feel like they cannot tell anyone or that no one will understand them. An accumulation of sadness, loss, anxiety, and negative emotions are buried. These remain unresolved in the background but do not disappear.

Comfort
The need for comfort manifests itself in multiple ways. Self-harmers are seeking to relieve tension from intense feelings. They want to escape from numbness, emptiness, depression, and feelings of worthlessness. It, then, becomes comforting to escape from reality. The pain helps them to create a new reality. They can deal with the reality of the pain from a cut. They cannot deal with pain from a betrayed family structure. The effect is depersonalization and dissociation from life circumstances.

Self-harm is also used as a way to obtain and maintain a loved one's attention and to influence the behavior of others. This is all a way to communicate to others one's need for comfort and a relationship.

Self-harm is also done in a continual effort to validate emotional pain. When people stuff emotions, they are subconsciously saying that they are not important enough to deal with. Those feelings are determined to be wrong or silly. Dealing with those emotions can then manifest itself in cutting.

Also, comfort can come in a biochemical response. A desire might be to obtain feelings of euphoria. Our bodies are naturally designed to respond to an injury with a burst serotonin, adrenaline, and other chemicals.

Control
Self-harmers have experienced terrible things in life that were out of their control. As a result, they want to do what they can to regain control (see addiction chart in Chapter 2). The pain and numbness they feel becomes muted for a short time when they self-harm because new pain is present. This is the substitutionary effect.

Our bodies have pain receptors that cause us to stop an action if it is painful. The self-harmer can continue through pain that should otherwise make them stop because the pain of their reality is far greater than the pain they are experiencing at the moment. They are trying to rid themselves of emotional pain by substituting physical pain.

<u>It takes great feelings of emotional pain to proceed through great feelings of physical pain.</u> This is an exercise of exerting a sense of control over one's body, something commonly found in cases of abuse.

Think of a candle. If you hold your hand to the flame, you recoil because of the pain. My friend is a fire fighter, and he says that his fear and pain become dulled when he sees someone's life in danger, and that enables him to run into the fire. A higher priority is now the concern.

The higher priority arises for the self-harmer to push through the natural reactions to pain because of other, more severe distress. The goal is pain itself. It is the dressing up of already existing pain and substituting it with another – remedying one type of pain with another type of pain, physical pain as a cure for emotional pain.

Further, self-harm has been a way to repress sexuality. This is seen in cases of incest and rape. Victims see themselves as the cause for their trauma and pain instead of the offender. They think this is a way to maintain an ideal family structure. Unwilling to expose the offender for the sake of the family, they take it out on themselves.

A healthy way to deal with hurt or pain is to talk about it. Verbally expressing hurts allows a person to move the traumatizing experience outside of themselves, where it can be directed, understood, shared, and put in the past. Substituting one pain for another only provides short-term relief (see the Addiction Chart in Chapter 2). It only adds to the pile of negative emotions.

"It's All My Fault"

Have you ever wondered how some people might come to the conclusion of thinking that the situation is their fault when the there is somebody who is obviously guilty? When a perpetrator is clearly at fault, why would a teenager say, "This is my fault!"

It is because this is a form of control. If I own the circumstance and say, "It's my fault," then I can figure out how fix to it. It gives me an illusion of control. "If my father thinks I'm stupid, then all I have to do is be smarter." "If I was molested because I was too fun and charming, then all I have to do is be more withdrawn."

The self-harmer struggles with an identity of defectiveness. But if they see how they are defective, they can try to fix it.

Once they have decided it is their fault then in their mind, they can try and own it and manage it. However, this leads them to destructive choices that will help them manage and numb the pain.

Self-harm, drugs, alcohol, pornography, and promiscuity are all destructive avenues people use to deal with pain. When they can't manage their emotions or their situations, then it leads them down into further destructive choices and mentalities. "I am a loser." "I am horrible." "I feel trapped." "Something is wrong with me."

Everyone is familiar with these feelings. People feel alone, like no one cares. Self-harm is just another manifestation of these feelings. When no one answers, they feel like they have to take care of themselves. It is an attempt at emotional management – a search for comfort.

But God hears us. He hears his children. He is the better remedy for our pain. He answers when we cry and lifts our burdened souls when we are overwhelmed. God holds us in his sanctuary under his care - even while we are broken, bloody, and crying.

Psalm 61:1-4
O God, listen to my cry! Hear my prayer!
From the ends of the earth
I cry to you for help
when my heart is overwhelmed.
Lead me to the towering rock of safety,
for you is my safe refuge,
a fortress where my enemies cannot reach me.
Let me live forever in your sanctuary,
safe beneath the shelter of your wings!

Chapter 5 - Understanding Family Dynamics

Lesson Overview
In this lesson, we will discuss the effects of a broken family system on a child.

The Role Reversal Effect
Self-injury is not just a result of a poor parenting style. Actually, every parent is imperfect and raises their children imperfectly. What we are talking about is a sheer failure to step into the parent role. Self-harm is often the result of a parent abandoning their God-given responsibility in their child's life.

When parents who are gripped by anxiety look to the child for emotional support, the "Role Reversal" effect occurs. This happens when parents give their child their emotional authority, and the child becomes the head of the family. The parent seeks validation. This causes a shift in power to the child, who now feels the burden to fill a role they know they are not ready to step into.

"Its not fair."
"I never had a childhood."
"I had to grow up quickly."
"I feel like I am the parent."

<u>A child needs the parent to be a parent, not the other way around</u>. With the child in power, the child has no sense of security. Children need authority figures in their lives. Without parental authority, they have no discernment in making decisions. Then are forced to formulate their own perception of reality based on their own values. One of the most detrimental things anyone can do to a child is to remove security, structure, and direction from them and to allow them to raise themselves.

A role reversal can happen in a number of ways. Parents might be chronically ill or disabled. They might suffer from a mental disorder. They might be addicted to alcohol or drugs. In all these cases the child might feel the need to be an emotional pillar for their parent – something that they themselves need.

The Triangulation Effect
A healthy relationship between the father and mother is essential to a child's upbringing. This is why the Bible sets up the family structure as it does. This is why divorce is so detrimental. When the relationship breaks down between parents, the child can be the target of either of the parent's aggression or frustrations. This is called the "Triangulation" effect.

Triangulation happens when one party feels like it is being outnumbered on the opposing side of two or more other parties. For example: Dad & Child vs. Mom… or Mom & Child vs Dad. The child will feel in the middle of two parents as the tipping point of power and control in the relationships. With the tremendous power and authority of choosing a side, a Role Reversal effect can occur.

This plays out in one of two ways: manipulation and blame.

The first is when one parent manipulates their child onto their side and against the other parent, putting the child in the middle and forcing him or her to choose a side. Forcing a child to choose to abandon their relationship with one parent in order to keep the other is cruel. A parent forces this choice because they are insecure. They want to be liked and loved more than the other parent. They want to be loved and valued more than they want the stability for the child.

The second way triangulation occurs is when the child becomes the target for aggression (caused by and intended for) the other parent. The parent blames the child. This burdens the child with guilt, shame, and fear. The child becomes guilt ridden and thinks that the marital desertion is their fault. They are shamed into painful humiliation, causing withdrawal. And now they fear rejection from a parent, which strikes them to the core of who they are in their formative years.

The Contradictory Fusion Effect

When a parent sends mixed signals of love and abuse, the "Contradictory Fusion" effect occurs. It is a blend of emotions a child feels when they are the victim of abuse from a family member that comes hypocritically packaged with the claim, "I love you." It is a confusing message of affection blended with pain.

The extreme need for acceptance in a child will lead to justifying the abuser's actions. It becomes a single emotion. A tangled web of feelings too complex to sort through is then accepted as one. Love, hate, right, wrong, justified, and abuse then all become one, and to cope with the stress of this blend the child may turn to self-harm.

A child cannot then properly discern what is right and wrong. They cannot balance their need for love with the abusive actions, so instead of correctly blaming the offender they incorrectly blame themselves. The child does not know how to deal with their situation outwardly, so inner turmoil sets in.

God's Family Structure

The Bible talks about how God has set up the family structure. It was meant to protect children and nurture them. But people are broken and sinful. Everyone knows there is no perfect family, but God designed the parental relationship to be the most powerful element in a child's development (whether present or not). However, it our earthly parents fail, we still have a perfect and loving father in heaven.

Our father is strong enough to protect us. He is engaged enough to teach us. He is tender enough to hug us. He is thoughtful enough to sympathize with us. He is close enough to cry with us. He is alive enough to walk with us.

Romans 8:15
The Spirit you received does not make you slaves, so that you live in fear again; rather, the Spirit you received brought about your adoption to sonship. And by him we cry, "Abba, Father."

Part Three
Understanding the Healing

Chapter 6 - Understanding Our Role

Lesson Overview
In this lesson we will discuss our role and how we should respond to different types self-harmers.

Victim vs. Chooser
In essence, you can view people who self-harm in one of two ways: a victim or a chooser.

The first is a victim. This person self-harms because terrible things have been done to them in their lives. They have had horrible experiences that were out of their control. This might include the death of a relative, abuse, neglect, abandonment, rejection, or bullying. They suffer from the effects of other people's misconduct. Because of this, they are driven to self-destructive behaviors.

The second is a chooser (the industry term is "agent") – someone who makes poor decisions that come back to bite them. This might include doing drugs, dropping out of school, stealing and getting caught. The reason they are in the situation they are is because of their own poor choices. This will then lead them into even more poor choices and more self-destructive behavior.

The only rational solution is to have two different responses to the two different types of self-harmers. To the victim, you love them and give them a hug. You tell them everything will be ok. To the chooser, you kick them in the butt and tell them to stop making bonehead choices.

The problem is that it is never that easy. It is never one or the other. Life is messy.

The truth is that kids often make bad choices because bad things happened to them. It's a ball of yarn of terrible choices with a painful story. Someone cuts because there is a story behind the blade. A kid acts out because of a lack of attention. So what do we do when life and choices are tangled up together in a mess like this? How do we position ourselves?

Attached vs. Detached

Much like deciding how much of a victim someone is and how much of a chooser someone is, we must make similar judgments for ourselves in responding to our kids and their needs. The spectrum for us becomes how emotionally attached vs. how emotionally detached we are. This is mainly due to personality types and temperaments.

Some will be more emotionally attached – more invested. They will tend to be more loving, more tender, and more compassionate. People who fall more on the attached side of the scale will find themselves more comforting and eager to extend themselves further. They see that showing love, care, comfort, and sympathy is the primary thing they have to offer.

The emotionally detached helper sees that the best way to help a self-harmer would be to offer advice and insight that would practically help them. People who intend to help and who fall into this camp might take more of a professional approach to their care for the self-harmer. They tend to be more thoughtful and introspective, more analytical of the situation. They would be more likely to see a more concrete solution to a self-harmer's life problems.

No camp is better than the other, but rather both can offer help. Now let's combine the two different camps of helpers with the two different types of self-harmers. This will show us how we can appropriately respond to any situation.

The Response Matrix

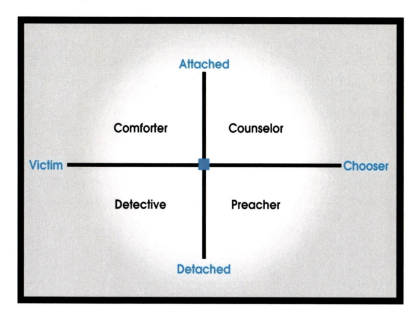

The horizontal line is the scale of whether or not we view our self-harmer is a victim or a chooser. The vertical line is the scale of whether or not we are more emotionally attached or detached. This is a general guide to how we would respond or should respond.

Which one are you most like?

Attached x Victim = The Comforter
The Comforter is the combination of perceiving a self-harmer as a victim with the personality of being more attached. This will lead the helper to act in a certain way that the others would not. The self-harmer will get a strong sense of love and encouragement from the Comforter.

Tears will be cried together, and when they hurt the Comforter feels it too.

Some weaknesses of this response quadrant is that it only provides a band aid. A hug doesn't really solve anything in the long run if no actions are taken. Comforters may even enable the self-harmer's actions. Furthermore, this quadrant is more prone to wear down your own personal relationships.

Attached x Chooser = The Counselor
The Counselor will acknowledge that the self-harmer is making mistakes in life and will want to speak truth and direction into the person's life. They will observe that they are getting into things that can be avoided, and they will teach wisdom to the self-harmer regarding their situation. Their aim is to teach the self-harmer life lessons in order that they might make better informed decisions.

A weakness the Counselor's approach is that one of the things that kids hate most is advice. Kids really don't respond well to advice in general. The weakness of this quadrant will be that sometimes the Counselor's words are received as empty and hollow.

Choosers x Detached = The Preacher
The Preacher is someone who sees the self-harmer as a chooser who puts themselves in the situations they are facing, while coming from a more detached approach. The Preacher would be there to confront them on things that no one else would call them out on. They would show them the error of their ways and hold them to a higher standard. They would be better able than the others to put structure and discipline in a place where there previously wasn't any.

Some weaknesses of this approach are that it can produce more shame instead of offering freedom and forgiveness. It can tend to make someone feel guilty and push them away, rather than bringing them closer by building a relationship with them. The Preacher's love and care for the self-harmer can feel more like a bludgeon to the side of the head.

Victim x Detached = The Detective
The Detective is someone who is detached enough to be analytical about the situation but sympathetic enough to realize that the self-harmer is a victim. They have a soft heart for someone with a problem that needs to be removed. When analyzing the victim's life, they want to tap into what the real core problem is and to remove it. The Detective is particularly adept at diagnosing and solving problems sympathetically.

A weakness of the Detective is that they tend to be impatient when seeking to solve problems. They have a tendency toward a lack of compassion and see the situation primarily as a mystery to be solved. They do not have much regard to the healing process but rather see an immediate physical or psychological problem to be quickly solved.

Combining All Four
<u>The true answer to how do we respond to a self-harmer's situation is that we must select the appropriate response depending on the situation</u>. Sometimes we are called to be more detached or attached despite our temperaments. The self-harmer is a complex blend of victim and chooser. It is up to us to sift through the mess and respond correctly. No easy answers here.

The Holy Spirit
The Christian Worldview attributes all four of the response angles to the Holy Spirit. The Holy Spirit comforts us in our valleys. He is there to counsel us when we need to learn. The Holy Spirit convicts us of our sin so that we might live the full life we were meant to live. And the Holy Spirit

investigates our hearts to see the true motivating factors behind our actions.

The Bible talks about how the Holy Spirit is in all of us and empowers us to do the ministry that we could never do on our own. With the power of the Holy Spirit, we can take on all the different roles we need to. This is important because there is often a feeling of inadequacy that comes when we hear the problems of someone who self-harms. Their stories can overwhelm us and leave us feeling insecure about our ability to help.

I remember plenty of times when I said something that was far beyond my own wisdom, and I shocked myself. I remember when I was more loving and compassionate than I normally am. I remember having a great idea or insight that I was not naturally prone to have.

The Holy Spirit is our "ace in the hole." He is the one that guides the healers and restores hurting. He is the one who changes lives, and we are the instruments of this great change. We can walk in confidence when we walk with the Holy Spirit.

1 Corinthians 12:7-11
Now to each one the manifestation of the Spirit is given for the common good. To one there is given through the Spirit a message of wisdom, to another a message of knowledge by means of the same Spirit, to another faith by the same Spirit, to another gifts of healing by that one Spirit, to another miraculous powers, to another prophecy, to another distinguishing between spirits, to another speaking in different kinds of tongues, and to still another the interpretation of tongues. All these are the work of one and the same Spirit, and he distributes them to each one, just as he determines.

Chapter 7 - Relational Recovery

Lesson Overview
In this lesson, we will talk about the road to recovery through a relationship.

Relational Pain, Relational Recovery
Most of the source of pain in a self-harmer's life is from a relationship gone bad – betrayal, neglect, abuse, etc. Therefore, it stands to reason that the only solution for a bad relationship in their life is a good relationship in their life – one that doesn't bring pain but joy. Instead of a relationship that brings chaos, a good relationship brings structure. This relationship fills abandonment with presence and care.

Most of the time we think the problem is the behavior. If we think the problem is the behavior, then we think the solution is to change the behavior. This does not help a self-harmer down the road to recovery in any way. It doesn't address their need for love. It doesn't deal with their past. This does not give them a sense of belonging. We must treat their situation with a relational response.

Kids will talk with a person they trust, not a person they are "supposed" to turn to. There are all kinds of hotlines and experts with degrees and certifications. In the end, however, kids do not care about your certification; they care about your character. They want someone with integrity and someone in their life who is trustworthy. If they see this in you, they will want to share their lives with you.

Kids don't care about what we know until they know that we care.

Three Things They Long for
There are three things that kids want and long for from the adults in their lives.
Availability. Authenticity. Acceptance.

Availability
They want you to be present. They want you to be near and with them. They are used to he feeling of abandonment and neglect. They are used to trying to have to vie for the attention of someone. We combat this emotion by just being available for them. Being there for them shows them that you care and that they are a priority. They have never felt like a priority to anyone before, but you can show them they are a priority to you.

Availability without boundaries can have negative effects on the relationship. Some might say, "Call me anytime, anywhere; I'll be there for you." Don't over promise. We are not omnipresent. If you make this promise, you might just get a call at 3:00 a.m. and not be able to answer. You might be in the shower, or your phone might be dead. In their eyes, this is a broken promise. You have gone back on your word. What they will see is what they have always seen. "I knew it. You're just like the other ones." Make an availability promise you can keep. Make it vast and open but not without your limitations in mind. No one is really available 24/7. If you overpromise, you set yourself up to be their personal messiah, which is only setting yourself up for failure.

Authenticity
They want you to be real and honest. They want to see that it is ok to feel the way they feel. Authenticity connects two people, and it is the basis of any relationship. Without authenticity, the relationship is doomed to fail. They want adults who can be truthful with them and speak life to them. They don't want someone who stays at a distance.

They want someone who is willing to share their life with them.

Authenticity without boundaries can have negative effects on the relationship. "Yeah I understand your addiction to porn because I'm really struggling too. The reason is because my marriage is crumbling, and my wife cheated on me." There is a danger to share too much information. This is done when the helper is dealing with their own anxieties and is seeking comfort from the one who needs help. This is a form of role reversal discussed in Chapter 5. A general principle of being authentic is to ask yourself if what you are saying will be beneficial to them. Do they need to hear it? Will it build them up? Their benefit is the purpose of you speaking, not yours.

Acceptance

This is a heartfelt need for everyone but especially true for someone who self-harms. They feel like they have never had unconditional acceptance. A self-harmer has always thought that if they do enough for someone, they will love them. In other words, they think they can earn acceptance. They think that their life is a mess and will be a barrier that keeps people from loving them, so they compensate for it. We can't be turned off by their mess. They get that feeling from everyone else. We must be willing to live life with them in their mess. No judgment, no condemnation, and no need to earn their acceptance. They need to be loved for who they are.

Acceptance without boundaries can have negative effects on the relationship. If we give too much acceptance, we might enter the realm of enabling. We do not want to come off as if we are allowing the negative behavior. We set them up for failure if we do. They want to be accepted for the life they have, but they also want someone to show them a better one. We need to get to the point where we can say, "I love you as you are, but I love you too much to let you stay there." This is why we build a relationship with them – so that we can earn the right to speak into their lives.

Prepare for the Long Haul
All three of these things take time to develop. A LONG TIME. Changing isn't easy. Breaking down an old identity and reestablishing a new identity is a long journey. A relationship can be broken in an instant, but it takes a lifetime to rebuild. They will need you to sacrifice for them. They will need you to stretch and extend for them. Be prepared to care for them the way Jesus would care for them.

You can do it! The Holy Spirit is with you and will empower you to carry out healing. But in order to help kids, we need to be healthy ourselves. And the Holy Spirit will ensure that we are cared for as well. Live a life of walking with the Holy Spirit, and that will be the best thing for you and for your loved ones. Live a life that is authentic and true. Be a person who is trustworthy. Be a mentor that emulates that lifestyle of Jesus Christ.

The Gospel is a Relationship
Living a life that is worthy of trust is important to them. Listen deeply, actively, and non-judgmentally. True healing happens in that type of relationship. This is why the good news of the Gospel is so important.

The power of the Gospel is in our relationship with Jesus Christ. He is always available to us. We see a person we can look to in Jesus as an example. He was humble and kind and worthy of our trust. In Jesus, God offers unconditional acceptance. We don't have to earn our right to be in a relationship with God. That right is given freely to us. In the book of Romans, the question is asked, "What can separate us from the love of God?" a few verses later the question is answered with a spectacular promise.

Romans 8:37-39
No, in all these things we are more than conquerors through him who loved us. For I am convinced that neither death nor life, neither angels nor demons, neither the present nor the future, nor any powers, neither height nor depth, nor anything else in all creation, will be able to separate us from the love of God that is in Christ Jesus our Lord.

Chapter 8 - Action Steps

Lesson Overview
In this lesson, we will combine everything we have learned and discuss five specific action steps you can take next. We will also look at six milestones we want to see in the life of the self-harmer.

Five Things You Must Do
You Must Affirm. You must affirm character traits rather than physical beauty or achievements to combat their low self-esteem. Affirm, encourage, and praise behaviors such as kindness, gentleness, tenderness, and thoughtfulness. Affirming physical aspects or accomplishments only drive them back towards conditional acceptance.

Powerful Statement: "I think one of my favorite things about you is that you are _____ (kind, thoughtful, generous)!"

You Must Listen. Cutters deal with stuffed emotions all the time. Actively listen to their story and what they are saying. Ask questions. Get engaged. The goal is to bring out how they feel so that they can deal with it externally.

Powerful Statement: "What is it like to be you? What's going on inside of you? What did you feel when that happened to you?"

You Must Be Present. Self-harmers deal with abandonment. Simply being available to them speaks volumes. It shows them they are not at the bottom of your priority list. It gives worth to someone who feels worthless.

Powerful Statement: "I am here for you. I am in your corner, cheering you on!"

You Must Accept. Cutters deal with a great sense that they are defective. Unconditional acceptance is so important to the rebuilding of their lives. They should not feel like they have to work to be in a relationship with you. Also, they should not feel like if they let you down, you might give up on them. Don't give up on them! Encourage them. They must see themselves as God sees in them. This starts with you.

Powerful Statement: "I know you feel this way about yourself, but I don't feel that way about you!"

You Must Speak Hope. Self-harmers deal with despair. Speak about a hopeful and positive future for them. The goal is to help them see a future after self-harm. Talk about life after self-harm and what it would be like. Inquire about what would they do on a normal day and how would they would teach someone else. Give them a reason and purpose for all their pain.

Powerful Statement: "You are going to be an awesome _____ (mom, dad, and mentor)!"

Settle in. Recovery is complicated. If possible, habitual self-injurers should be referred to a trained and qualified professional therapist. But you will still have a huge role in their life.

Six Milestones: Things You Want Them to Say/Feel

The following is a series of statements that can serve as signposts on the road to recovery. Recovery is a journey of rediscovery. This cannot be rushed, and you should expect setbacks, but the important thing is to never give up! Strive for progress, not perfection.

Progress and success happens when the self-harmer says...

1. "My story matters. Someone is listening to me." - We get them to this milestone by listening to them.

2. "The emotions in my story are important." - They are moving past seeing only the facts, timeline and characters as important in their story, which leads to a stuffing of emotions.

3. "The way I've been feeling is legitimate/valid." - We get them to this milestone by telling them that we would have felt the same way in similar circumstances. The goal here is getting them to acknowledge that they are the victim.

4. "My desire to manage my pain is normal and healthy." - We get them here by agreeing with them that no one wants to feel that way all the time.

5. "What I am doing now is destructive." - **This is the turning point**. Reaching this point requires love, care, and a relationship that you can use to speak life into them. This cannot be rushed.

6. "I must be willing to explore healthier options" - This is a place of healing and hope.

Recovery is Repentance

The essence of healing should start with repentance. You might say, "Repent?! Of what? What do they have to repent of?! Cutting?! That's a sin!?"

The problem is we tend to define sin as behavioral. It becomes nothing more than swearing, drinking, and cutting. If we keep a definition of sin that is merely behavioral, then the only option is that the definition of repentance becomes downgraded into a change in behavior. Repentance is much more. It is a change in the direction they are moving toward. If we keep saying repentance is, "Don't do that," the Gospel loses the essence of its power. The power of the Gospel is relational.

True Biblical repentance is not just a turning from something, but to something. It is not behavioral. It is relational. We need to recognize that the call of the Gospel is to turn to someone. It's returning to the life we were meant to live in relationship with God. It's about restoring a relationship. The expressions of sin and self-harm will take care of themselves.

Isaiah 55:6-7
Seek the LORD while he may be found; call upon him while he is near; let the wicked forsake his way, and the unrighteous man his thoughts; let him return to the LORD, that he may have compassion on him, and to our God, for he will abundantly pardon.

Epilogue

Most of us are reading this book because we have discovered that someone we love has been harming themselves. Feelings of guilt, frustration, worry, and confusion might settle in. You may want to help but just didn't even know where to begin. I hope this book helped shed some light on how you might understand the person behind the behavior. I hope you now feel more confident to be able to help someone who is suffering.

I hope you are able to see that his behavior is beatable. I want to encourage you to continue to walk with your loved one and to not give up on them. It will be hard, and the journey will be long, but you will be a shining light in their life that is engulfed in darkness.

My best advice: The closer you walk with Jesus, the better you will be able to help them. He has the power to change lives.

The Gospel speaks to every aspect of the suffering of his children. I believe that true healing is only offered in the Christian Worldview. God enters into our lives and isn't afraid of our mess. Jesus suffered so that we don't have to. On the cross, he took our guilt and shame and died with it. Three days later he rose from the grave, and he gives us his Holy Spirit.

With him we are empowered us to take our mess and turn it into a message.

1 Peter 2:24
He himself bore our sins in his body on the tree, that we might die to sin and live to righteousness. By his wounds you have been healed.

I'd Love to Hear from You!

Thank you for reading! I'd love to hear your stories of success through suffering.

Additionally, as an author, I regard the feedback of my readers highly. When considering a book, people use reviews to decide whether or not to read it.

If you have enjoyed this book and have found value to the things discussed, please consider helping others make an informed decision and share this book with someone because it might help them too!

God Bless,
Aaron Mamuyac

About the Author

Aaron is a preacher, teacher, youth worker, and Christ follower. He has been serving in youth ministry for 10 years at Sunlight Community Church in South Florida. Aaron specializes in gospel-centered teaching to a modern cultural context and seeks to "bridge the gap between Christ and Culture."

Other Books

15 Minute Hospital Visit: 7 Simple Things You Need to Know for Quick and Effective Visitation to Show Pastoral Care

Unfortunately, if you are in any kind of ministry work, tragedy will strike, and you will eventually have to visit someone in the hospital.

The truth is that visiting people in hospitals is much easier than you have been led to believe. In fact, most people get intimidated by the thought of doing hospital visits because they are uncomfortable and don't know what to say.

I am going to share with you the simple 7-step process that I go through that has allowed me to not only get over my fears of doing hospital visits but actually enjoy them.

Business Inquiry
aaron@sunlightcc.org
www.aaronmamuyac.com

Sunlight Community Church
www.sunlightcc.org

Made in the USA
Columbia, SC
30 January 2023